All About Snakes and Lizards

by Helen Gregory

Table of Contents

Consultant:
Adria F. Klein, Ph.D.
California State University, San Bernardino

capstone classroom
Heinemann Raintree • Red Brick Learning
division of Capstone

Reptiles

Snakes and lizards are reptiles.
A reptile is a kind of animal.
They are alike in many ways.

Reptiles have backbones and their bodies are covered in dry scales.

All reptiles are cold-blooded. They need to warm themselves in the sun.

They need to cool themselves in the shade.

Tongues

Reptiles don't have noses,
so they use their tongues to smell.
The tongue flicks out to pick up
a smell.

The tongue tells the mouth if a smell is an enemy or a nice meal.

Shedding

Some reptiles shed their skin as they grow.
New skin grows underneath the old skin.

The skin of a snake sheds all at once.
It looks like a sock coming off.
Lizards shed a little at a time.

Differences

Snakes and lizards are different in many ways.

Most lizards have legs.

Snakes do not have legs.
They bend their bodies back
and forth to move.

Most lizards have eyelids.
Their eyelids open and shut.

Snakes do not have eyelids. Their eyes are always open. A clear scale covers their eyes to protect them.

Lizards and snakes hear in different ways. Lizards have ear openings. Snakes do not have ear openings. They feel the ground moving.

Some reptile babies hatch from eggs.

Other reptiles give birth to live young.
How many baby snakes can you count?